CREEPY CRAWLIES

Tiny Creatures, Amazing Powers

SCRIBO

Richard
and
Louise Spilsbury

Contents

Creepy-crawlies

Ants, bees, and dragonflies are definitely all creepy-crawlies. But to be more scientific, they're also insects. The scariest thing about insects is just how numerous they are. There are more than a million known species of insect, which is more than any other class of animal. In fact, insects alone actually account for more than half of the world's total population of different life forms!

But what exactly is an insect? And how would you know if you found one? Insects are invertebrates, which means that they do not have spines. They can be identified by the fact that they all have exoskeletons, which is an external skeleton or shell that protects the organs, as well as a three-part body, compound eyes, three pairs of jointed legs, and antennae.

Spiders are also very creepy and very crawly, but they're arachnids, not insects. An arachnid is also a type of invertebrate, but it has eight legs instead of six and is generally even scarier!

Each of the four main chapters in this book focuses on a different species of creepy-crawly, exploring how they're put together and what they do to survive. So read on to discover more...if you dare!

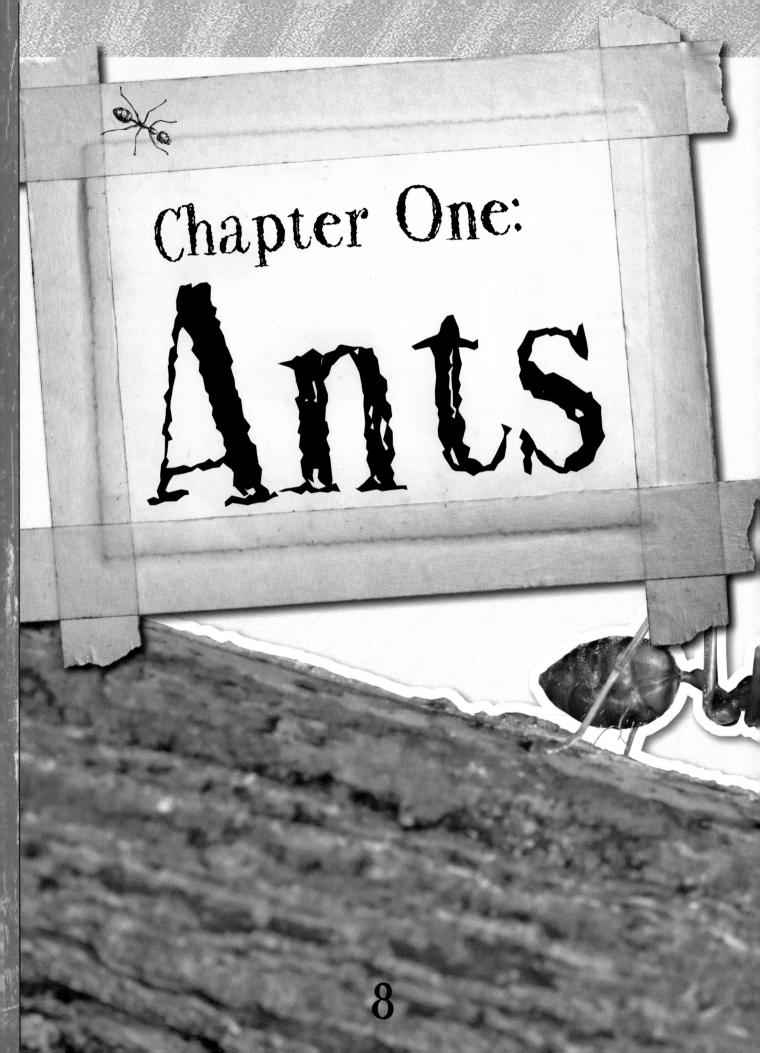

Chapter One:
Ants

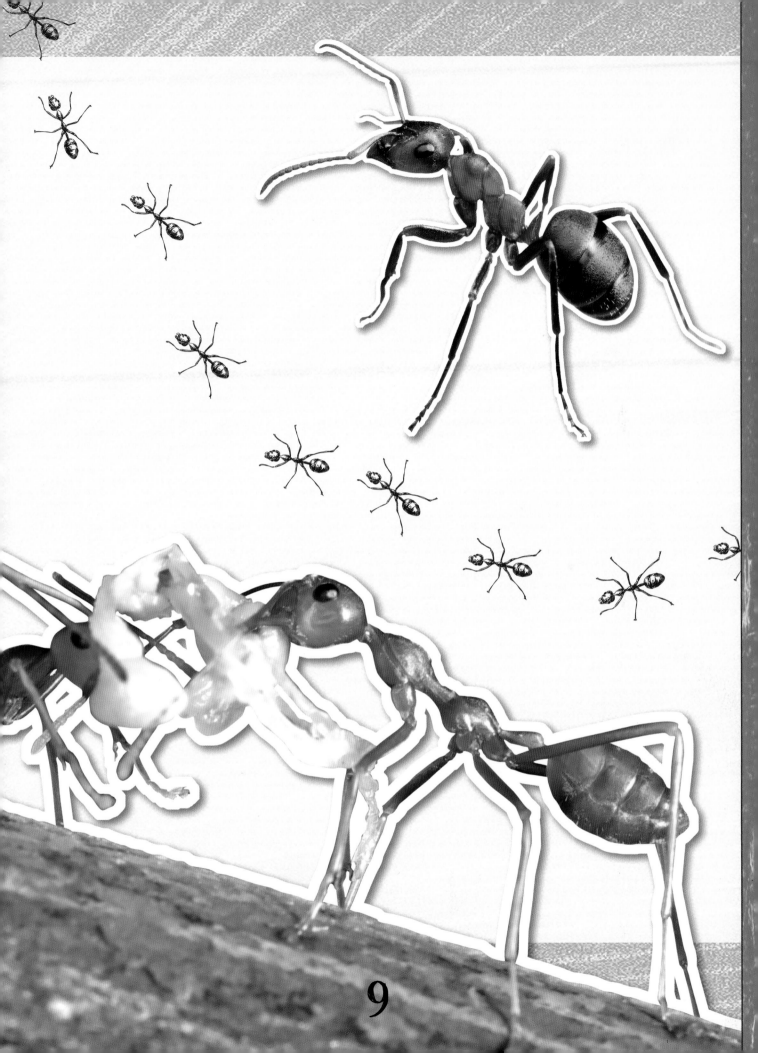

9

Ants

There are about 100 trillion ants living in every corner of our planet, except the freezing Arctic and Antarctic regions. These little insects are divided up into 13,000 different **species** or distinct types. Some ants are 2 inches (5 cm) long, while others are so small that 32 ants in a row would measure only 1 inch (2.5 cm) long. Ants can be black, brown, yellow, green, or blue.

Up close, with their big jaws, ants look pretty scary, but the scariest thing about ants is that they always live in a group or **colony**. An ant colony can consist of millions of insects that attack anything in their path. There are colonies with only tens of insects, too. Not all ants in a colony look the same. Most are worker ants that do many different jobs for the colony, including collecting food. Soldier ants are the colony's army. They attack if the colony or nest is threatened. Queens are the most important ants in any colony. These females lay eggs that will hatch into new colony members.

This is a worker ant. In a colony, worker ants tend to the other ants, including the queen. They also build nests.

Soldier ant

Queen ant

Ants in a colony look different because they have different jobs to do for the survival and success of their group.

11

The Body

Like other insects, an ant's body is made up of three parts, or sections. The head is used to figure out what is around the ant. It has eyes, mouthparts, and antennae (**jointed** parts for sensing). The head is joined to the **thorax**, to which the legs are attached. The thorax is attached by a narrow waist to the **abdomen**. This is where the ant digests its food.

Superpowers

Once a year, some of the colony's male and young female queen ants develop wings. On a warm afternoon, they swarm from their nest and take to the air. The flight is all about **reproduction**. Queens release a **chemical** to attract males, and **mate** with the fastest fliers. All the males die after mating, but each queen flies to a different place to start a new colony. Then, they bite off their wings because they no longer need them. If humans had this superpower, they would chew off their legs because they had reached their destination!

Leg

Thorax

Eye

Mouth

Antenna

Abdomen

Ants have a distinct shape with a large head and abdomen, and a thinner thorax.

13

The Abdomen

An ant's abdomen is rounded in shape and covered in short bristles. Inside are many organs, which are important for a range of life processes. For example, tubes called tracheae move air to different parts of the body for respiration (breathing). Queens produce eggs in the abdomen for reproduction. The abdomen also contains two stomachs. One, called the crop, is for storing food for the colony. The other is smaller, and is used for storing an ant's own food.

Superpowers

The honeypot ant can super-size! These ants live in deserts and other dry places where food is plentiful only in the wet season. In the wet season, special, large workers, called repletes, are fed so much sugary liquid by the other ants that their abdomens swell up to the size of cherries. In the dry season, other ants in the colony stroke the repletes to make them vomit some of their food store. If an average man's stomach swelled up that much, he would have a waist size of 17.7 feet (5.4 meters)!

Abdomen

Ants have **glands** in their abdomen that make chemical smells, which other ants recognize. They press their abdomen while they walk, to leave a scent trail that other ants can follow.

If ants look like they are kissing, they are actually feeding each other! One spits up food from its crop in the abdomen into the other's mouth.

Waist

Some ants tap their abdomen on the colony nest to warn ants inside of danger.

The Head

An ant's brain is inside its head. The brain is about the size of a pinhead, which is quite big for an insect. Ants use their brain to process all the information from their antennae, eyes, and other **sense organs**, to understand and remember things about the world around them. Ants see by using their two large **compound eyes**, which can detect movement but not very clear images. They also have tiny **simple eyes** on their head that can tell if it is light or dark.

Superpowers

Ants are clever for their size because their brains are so big. Their brain mass is one-seventh of their body mass. An average human weighs 137 pounds (62 kilograms). If humans had the same brain-mass to body-mass **ratio**, then an average brain weight would be nearly 20 pounds (9 kilograms). Imagine how big the person's head would need to be!

16

The ants with the clearest
vision are bull ants.
They can see objects up
to 3 feet (1 meter) away.

Simple eye

Compound eye

Mouthpart

17

The Antennae

Imagine having two bendy things sticking out of your forehead to smell with and to touch things. An ant's antennae are covered with tiny sense organs that can identify chemicals in the air. They can also feel air **currents**, **vibrations**, and textures. A sense of smell is important for recognizing other ants. If an ant has the same smell of the colony, the other ants welcome it. If the smell is different, then they may fight.

Superpowers

Fire ants dig narrow tunnels to make underground nests. They spend much of their lives moving through these tunnels, avoiding bumping into ants coming the other way. Sometimes tunnels collapse, but the ants never stumble because they use their antennae like grippers to grab on to the tunnel walls. If humans had this superpower, they would have stabilizers attached to their head. They would never fall over or bump into anything. Walking in a crowded place would never be the same again!

18

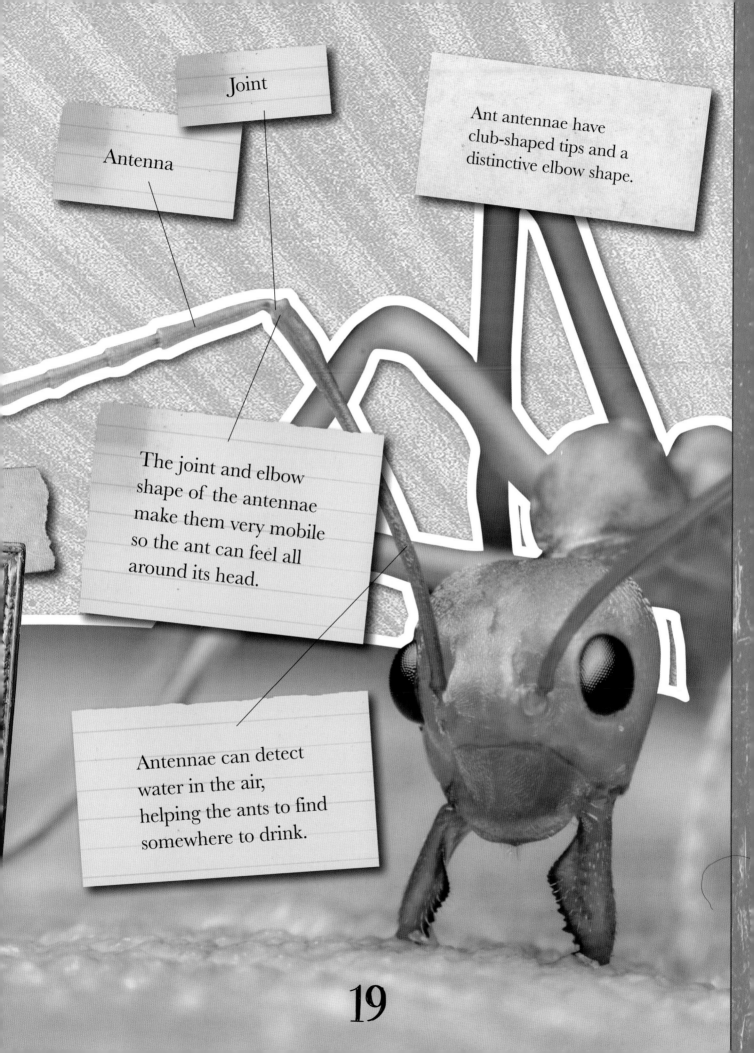

Joint

Antenna

Ant antennae have club-shaped tips and a distinctive elbow shape.

The joint and elbow shape of the antennae make them very mobile so the ant can feel all around its head.

Antennae can detect water in the air, helping the ants to find somewhere to drink.

19

The Mouth

Up close, the scariest looking parts of an ant are its mouthparts. Ants have strong, jagged, triangular jaws called mandibles. Mandibles can grip like pliers, pierce like daggers, and dig like spades. Ants use their mandibles to attack and eat prey. They use them to carry food or water droplets back to other ants in the colony. They also use them to fetch mud or make a substance like papier maché to build their nest. Ants' other mouthparts include lips that can taste food.

Antenna

Mandible

An ant grips things with its mandibles, using them rather like hands.

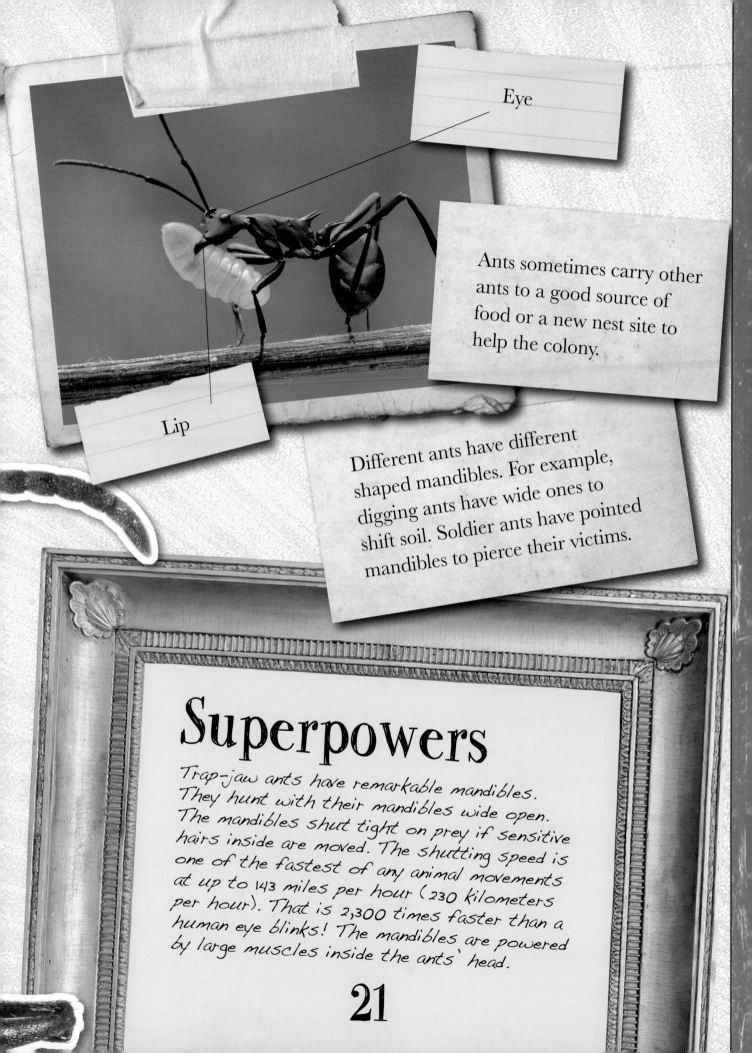

Eye

Ants sometimes carry other ants to a good source of food or a new nest site to help the colony.

Lip

Different ants have different shaped mandibles. For example, digging ants have wide ones to shift soil. Soldier ants have pointed mandibles to pierce their victims.

Superpowers

Trap-jaw ants have remarkable mandibles. They hunt with their mandibles wide open. The mandibles shut tight on prey if sensitive hairs inside are moved. The shutting speed is one of the fastest of any animal movements at up to 143 miles per hour (230 kilometers per hour). That is 2,300 times faster than a human eye blinks! The mandibles are powered by large muscles inside the ants' head.

The Legs

Ants are fast and nimble movers. Their six, jointed legs are tipped with tiny claws that give them great grip, even on smooth surfaces. Ants rarely lose balance because of the way their legs move. At any one time, three legs are in contact with the floor. As one lifts up, another touches the ground, so they are stable like a three-legged stool. An ant's front legs have special brushes of hairs on them that the ant uses to clean its **exoskeleton**.

Superpowers

Sahara desert ants live in one of the hottest places on Earth. They have extra-long legs that raise them above sand as hot as 140°F (60°C) while they move around in search of dead insects to eat. These ants search up to 328 feet (100 meters) away but always return to their nests because they can remember exactly how many steps they have taken. This is like a person counting the steps on a 28-mile (45-kilometer) trip!

22

Leg

Joint

The end segment, or tarsus, has claws to help the ant to climb and to stop slipping.

Like other insects, ants have legs with five parts or segments connected by joints.

23

The Stinger

An ant's **stinger** is the pointed bit at the end of its abdomen. On some types of ant, the stinger is the shape of a needle. This is used to inject **venom** under the skin of **prey** or any animal that is threatening the ant. In other ants, the stinger is nozzle shaped to shoot venom into the eyes or onto the skin of **predators**.

Superpowers

The most terrifying ants are jumper ants and bulldog ants. These insects can kill people. They are very aggressive and have no fear of humans. They bite with their long mandibles and then curl their abdomen to deliver a venomous sting. The venom is extremely painful and makes the victim's flesh feel as though it is on fire. It can also cause death within 15 minutes, usually in people who are **allergic** to the venom.

24

The chemicals in ant venom, including **formic acid**, are made in glands inside the abdomen.

Some birds, such as thrushes, stretch their wings and stamp on ant nests so that the ants come out and spray formic acid on them. The acid does not damage the birds but it kills **mites** hiding among the birds' feathers.

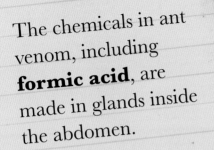

Stinger

Abdomen

Ant venom can be 20 times more poisonous than a honeybee's.

Weaver Ants

Ants make different types of nests including underground ones. However, the most remarkable is the nest of the weaver ant. Weaver ant workers make nests by bending leaves together. Some ants bite onto leaf edges and others link legs together with their claws. Many workers unite to pull the leaf edges together. Then, other workers carefully hold ant **larvae** in their jaws and tap them with their antennae. The larvae then produce silk to stick the leaves together.

Weaver ant workers have very strong jaws to grip leaves. They also use them to bite any animals trying to get near their nests.

Worker

Silk

Weaver ants usually make their soccer ball sized leaf nests in the forests of Australia and Southeast Asia.

Mandibles

Superpowers

Weaver ants are the weightlifting champions of the ant world. They have long strong legs that can lift up to 100 times their own weight. The strongest human weightlifters can lift only twice their own weight. If people were this strong, they could carry a full minibus.

27

Thorn Ants

Animals climbing onto or trying to feed on some tropical acacia trees better watch out! Acacia trees have big thorns with a swollen base that may have a nasty surprise inside. Thorn ants live in the hollow insides and are ready to stream out to attack with their stingers. The ants defend the tree because the acacia's leaf stalks supply a sweet liquid, called nectar, which the ants like to eat.

Thorn

Ant

Leaf

Thorn ants defend acacia trees from all kinds of leaf nibblers, from giraffes to bugs.

Superpowers

Thorn ants are tree surgeons, too! Different types of thorn ant may compete for the same tree, so the ants that occupy one tree stop other types from getting onto it. They use their mandibles to trim off the buds at branch tips. This stops the tree growing outward toward neighboring trees so that other ants cannot climb across.

Driver Ants

One of the scariest of all ant tales is about driver ants that kill people by swarming over them in death squads. This is not true, but driver ants are still a scary sight. They travel in columns measuring up to 328 feet (100 meters) long and more than 3.2 feet (1 meter) wide through African forests. A column may contain 20 million ants. They usually eat anything small in their path, from worms to insects, but occasionally they may eat bigger animals such as snakes or even horses.

Superpowers

Driver ants have fearsome mandibles. They are very strong with jagged edges that slice through the flesh of their victims. The jaws remain locked together, even if the head becomes detached from the body. Some people living in African forests utilize this when they get cut and are far from a hospital. They find driver ants, pinch the edges of the cut together, and hold the ants to it. The ants' mandibles staple the wound together.

30

Soldiers form the edge of the column so they can defend the worker ants in the middle.

Worker ants in the column carry food, eggs, and larvae.

Driver ant colonies live in one place for a few days and then move on in search of more food.

Driver ant columns may not be that fast at 0.009 miles per hour (0.014 kph)—but that is not bad considering these ants average just 0.1 inches (3 mm) long.

That's Scary!

People are outnumbered by ants on the planet. For each human there are several thousand ants. In some places, there are enormous colonies of ants underground, stretching for hundreds of miles across. Powerful brains, strong mandibles, stingers, and antennae are some of the body parts that have helped ants become so widespread. The way that jobs are split up between workers, soldiers, and queens in colonies, and they way that ants communicate to coordinate these jobs, are reasons for their success.

In some places, ants are scary pests that can damage houses and sting people and pets. In general, ants are very useful. They kill pests on food crops and insects that can harm people. Ants help to eat up sick and dead animals, and food waste. When they dig into soil, they spread **organic matter** and air through it, making the soil fertile and helping plants to grow. Some ants **pollinate** flowers, helping plants to make seeds. So, the scariest thing about ants is how much our planet needs them to remain healthy.

Some ants are survival experts that escape floods by forming rafts and bridges! Changes in the Earth's weather patterns from **climate change** could still threaten ant populations.

Leafcutter ants bite off parts of leaves to take into their nest, where they are turned into compost to grow mushrooms for the colony to eat!

Chapter Two:
Bees

Bees

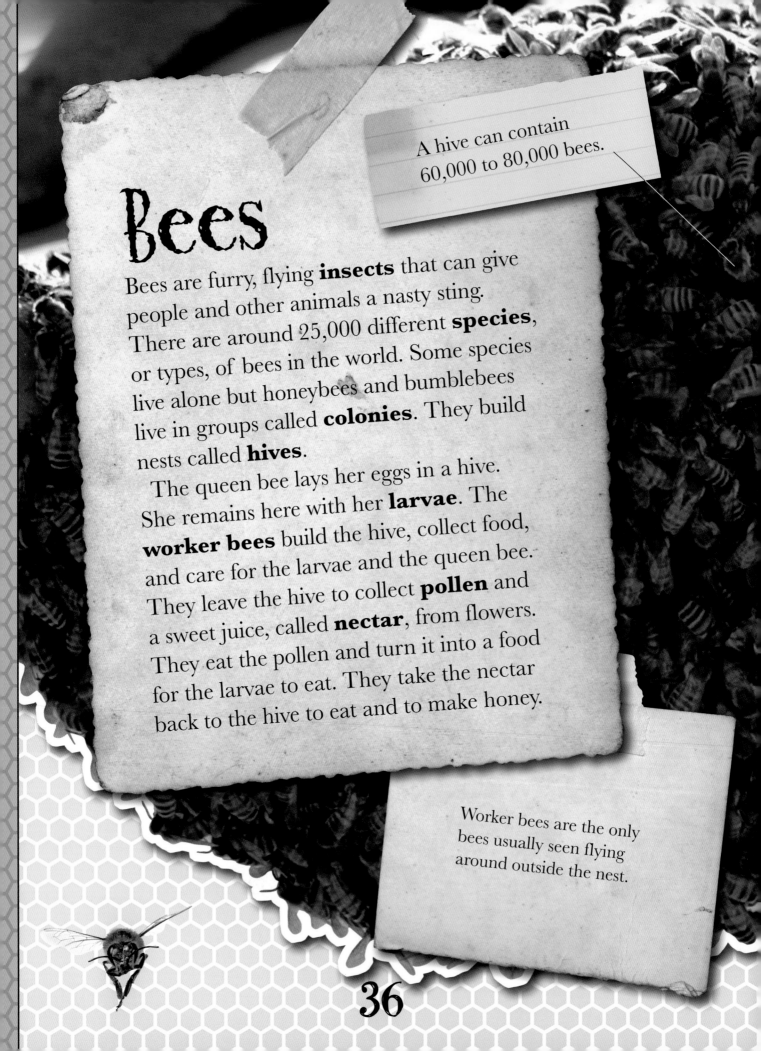

A hive can contain 60,000 to 80,000 bees.

Bees are furry, flying **insects** that can give people and other animals a nasty sting. There are around 25,000 different **species**, or types, of bees in the world. Some species live alone but honeybees and bumblebees live in groups called **colonies**. They build nests called **hives**.

The queen bee lays her eggs in a hive. She remains here with her **larvae**. The **worker bees** build the hive, collect food, and care for the larvae and the queen bee. They leave the hive to collect **pollen** and a sweet juice, called **nectar**, from flowers. They eat the pollen and turn it into a food for the larvae to eat. They take the nectar back to the hive to eat and to make honey.

Worker bees are the only bees usually seen flying around outside the nest.

Most bees have black and yellow stripes. These colors send a warning to other animals that bees can give them a painful sting.

37

The Body

Like other insects, the bee's body is made up of three main parts: the head, **thorax,** and **abdomen**. The body is covered in a hard outer coat, called an **exoskeleton**, which protects its insides. The bee's muscles are attached to the inside of the exoskeleton. The thick fuzzy hair on its body helps to keep it warm in cold weather. Pollen sticks to the bee's hair when it lands in a flower.

Superpowers

When a honeybee finds food, it tells other workers in the hive where to find it by doing a "bee dance." By flying in a circle or a figure-of-eight pattern and waggling its body, it can indicate the direction, distance, size, and quality of the food source. The food can be up to 3 miles (5 km) away. Imagine being able to communicate all that with a waggle of your hips!

As the bee dances, it waggles its abdomen to indicate how far away the flowers are.

When a food source is very close to the hive, the bee's dance is performed by moving in circles.

The angle of the bee's dance, in relation to the sun, tells other bees the direction of the food.

Bees can also use their waggle dance to tell other bees if there are any dangerous **predators** near the food source.

39

The Abdomen

The bee's abdomen contains two stomachs. One stomach is used to **digest** nectar. The second stomach is a honey sac that is used to carry nectar back to the hive. A bee's stinger is at the end of its abdomen. This sharp stinger pierces the skin and delivers **venom** into the victim's body. A bee will sting only to protect its colony or when it is frightened.

Honeybees sting only once. They die afterward because the stinger remains stuck inside the victim's skin and pulls out part of the bee's abdomen as the bee flies away.

The honeybee stinger is hollow and pointed, like a needle.

The stinger has two rows of saw-toothed hooks or blades to cut through the victim's skin.

The stinger hooks are angled. Once they are in a victim's body, they are hard to pull out.

Superpowers

The abdomen holds the secret to another bee superpower. Bees can find their way in the dark because substances inside their abdomen can sense the Earth's **magnetic field**. If humans had this superpower, it would be like having a built-in compass that they could use to navigate by. People would never need a map again.

41

The Antennae

The **antennae** are found on the bee's head between its eyes. The antennae can do many amazing things. They are packed with **sense organs** that can smell, taste, and feel. They can smell flowers and taste food. They sense the **vibrations** in the air made by bees when they dance. They also pick up the scents or smells that bees use to communicate. Antennae can sense wind direction and speed, so bees can work out how to fly faster, and how and where to land.

Superpowers

Some scientists think bees use their right antenna to tell the difference between bees from their own colony and those from another hive. Humans would have to be mind readers to be able to tell everything about someone without even speaking to them.

The many tiny hairs on the antennae are sensors, which detect scent and vibrations.

42

Bees have two antennae to figure out which direction a smell comes from and how far away it is. If a smell is stronger to one antenna than the other, it means the smell is closer to that side.

Bumblebees and honeybees have a **joint** in their antennae. This joint enables the antennae to bend in different directions.

The antennae usually have 12 or 13 segments.

The Eyes

If you look at a close-up of a bee's face, you can see five eyes staring back at you. A bee has three **simple eyes** and two **compound eyes**. The three simple eyes look like shiny bumps and they act as light sensors. They help the bee to see the sun, even when clouds are hiding it. The bee uses its eyes to spot brightly colored flower petals.

The simple eyes are arranged in a triangular pattern on the top of the head.

Superpowers

Bees can see things that are invisible to humans, including **ultraviolet (UV) light**. Many petals have ultraviolet lined patterns on them that guide the bees toward the flower's nectar stores. Bees can see these patterns clearly but humans cannot see them at all.

The compound eyes are made up of hundreds of little hexagonal units called **ommatidia**.

44

Each ommatidia has its own **lens**. The images it collects combine with the other lenses to form one whole picture.

The ommatidia are packed closely together but each one looks in a slightly different direction.

A bee's eyes cover most of the surface of its head.

45

The Mouth

Up close, a bee's mouthparts might look scary, but they are very useful. Inside the bee's mouth, fat mixes with saliva (spit) and other ingredients, such as soil or pollen, to make wax. It uses the wax to build the hexagonal cells that fit together to make a hive. A bee uses its stretchy tongue to drink and lick up nectar, honey, or water, and to pass on liquid to other bees.

Mandible

The **mandibles** are the bee's strong jaws. It uses them to cut and shape wax, to feed the larvae and the queen, to clean the hive, to fight, to groom, and to eat pollen.

Labial palp

Maxilla

The bee's long tongue has a hairy tip to help it to lap up food and water. It curls up when not in use.

Tongue

The tongue folds up into the labial palp and maxilla when not in use.

Superpowers

A bumblebee's tongue is amazing. It can reach up to 0.8 inches (2 cm) long when fully stretched, which is as long as its body. If a six-foot-tall man had a tongue like this, it would be more than one yard (92 cm) long. With a tongue as long as his arm, imagine how quickly he could lap up a drink!

47

The Wings

Bees use their wings to fly and can travel at a speed of around 16 miles per hour (25 kph). Their wings can beat 200 to 230 times per second. Bees also use their wings to keep the hive at a steady temperature. If the hive is too hot, the bees at the entrance flap their wings to waft in cool air.

Bee wings are transparent but they can look silvery when light strikes them at an angle.

Superpowers

Bees have incredible flying power. Each bee usually flies about 1 mile (1.6 km) from the hive each day, but they can fly up to 5 miles (8 km) to collect food. That means a big colony flies a distance equivalent to traveling as far as the moon every day!

48

Bee wings beat very fast so they can fly quickly and hover in one spot.

The front and back wings have hooks. The wings hook together so that they can beat as one when the bee is flying. The wings unhook and fold away when the bee is not flying.

The buzzing sound made by bees is actually the sound of their wings beating quickly.

49

The Legs

When they land on flowers, bees walk toward nectar stores and pollen. They also use their legs to help them to shape soft wax into the cells of their **honeycomb**. Bees have a groove on their legs that can be rubbed over their antennae to clean off pollen and dust, ensuring that the sensitive antennae keep working properly.

These hairs can form a basket for collecting pollen.

This is a press that helps the bee to pack pollen into the pollen baskets.

In the summer, a worker bee can carry two big pouches full of golden pollen on its legs.

This small groove is used to remove pollen from the bee's antennae.

The claws help a bee to grip surfaces and hold things.

Superpowers

A bee's back legs carry pollen to the hive. They use them to brush pollen onto hairless patches. These patches on the legs are surrounded by stiff hairs that form a basket. When a bee's legs are loaded with pollen and it has a stomach full of nectar, its cargo equals its own body weight. An airplane can take off only with a cargo of up to a quarter of its weight!

51

Queen Bee

Most hives have only one queen. The queen **mates** with male bees called drones, who live only for a short time and have no other job to do for their colony. The queen bee lays eggs and releases scents called **pheromones**. Only the bees in the queen's hive can smell these. The pheromones tell the bees that their queen is still alive and that all is well in the hive.

A queen bee is much bigger than a worker bee. However, her brain is smaller because her only job is to lay eggs.

Superpowers

A queen can lay about one egg every 20 seconds. In summer, a queen lays about 2,000 eggs, day and night. That means she lays her own body weight in eggs every 24 hours. If humans had that many babies, there would not be enough room on the planet for everyone to live.

If a queen bee dies, the workers create a new queen by choosing a young larva and feeding it a special food, called royal jelly, to make it grow into a queen bee.

Queen bee

Pheromones are such an efficient way of communicating that if a queen leaves the hive, all the bees in the colony know about it within 15 minutes.

Leafcutter Bees

Leafcutter bees live alone. They are so named because they cut leaves to build their nests in the holes found in rotting wood or plant stems. A leafcutter bee uses its mandibles to bite off pieces of leaf. It uses these pieces to create cell walls inside a barrel-shaped nest. It collects pollen and nectar to put inside each cell along with the larvae, so that they have enough food to grow into adults.

Leafcutter bees are black and about the size of a honeybee.

The underside of the abdomen often looks yellow because pollen is carried on stiff hairs there, rather than on their legs.

Superpowers

After cutting a piece of leaf, leafcutter bees fly back to the nest, clutching the leaf to the underside of their body. They are strong enough to carry a piece of leaf as big, if not bigger, than themselves. Just imagine if you walked around all day carrying objects bigger than yourself.

Leafcutter bees cut very neat circles or ovals from the edges of leaves. These measure about 0.75 inches (1.9 cm) in diameter.

Killer Bees

Africanized honeybees are known as killer bees because they are so scary! They behave normally when they are hunting for food but if they sense that their colony is in danger, they will defend it ferociously. When a large swarm of killer bees attacks people or animals it can kill because the swarm delivers up to 2,000 stings at once.

Killer bees are dangerous. While only about one in ten honeybees might attack to defend their hive, the whole colony of Africanized honeybees will attack if its hive is disturbed. By disturbing a honeybee colony you might get a few stings, but if you disturb an Africanized colony, you will get hundreds of stings!

Superpowers

Killer bees are deadly. When they sting, a chemical alarm is also given off. This alerts the other bees in their colony to danger and makes them swarm and attack. Killer bees react to disturbances ten times faster than European honeybees, and they will chase people up to a quarter of a mile (0.4 km) before they stop!

Once disturbed, colonies may stay on alert for up to 24 hours, attacking people and animals that they find near the hive.

56

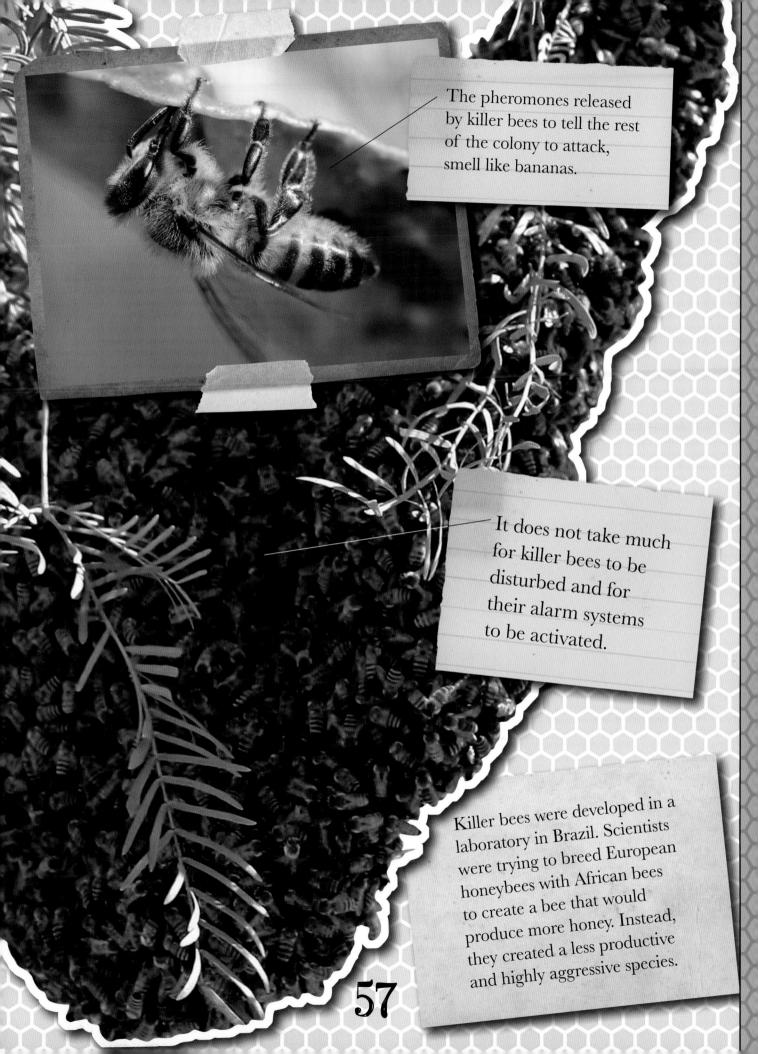

The pheromones released by killer bees to tell the rest of the colony to attack, smell like bananas.

It does not take much for killer bees to be disturbed and for their alarm systems to be activated.

Killer bees were developed in a laboratory in Brazil. Scientists were trying to breed European honeybees with African bees to create a bee that would produce more honey. Instead, they created a less productive and highly aggressive species.

57

That's Scary!

The truly scary thing about bees is that they are dying out. In the United States, more than half of all honeybee nests have disappeared. Some bees are dying because of **climate change**. As parts of the world become hotter, the heat is killing bees. Bees are also dying because trees are cut down and countryside is cleared, leaving fewer places for nests and fewer flowers to visit.

Bees make honey and **pollinate** plants. They mix nectar and saliva in their mouths to make a liquid that turns into honey in the hive cells. They make two to three times more honey than they need, so people can take some to eat. When bees move between flowers, they transfer pollen between the male and female parts of different flowers, allowing plants to grow seeds and fruit.

Superpowers

We need a lot of bees to make the honey we eat. Most worker bees live for about six weeks and make around one-twelfth of a teaspoon of honey. The bees in one colony have to fly about 55,000 miles (88,514 km) to make just 1 pound (0.4 kg) of honey—that is nearly seven times around the world!

58

Bees are vital—we need them. They pollinate three-quarters of the world's most important crops.

Chapter Three: Dragonflies

61

Dragonflies

Dragonflies are large, winged **insects** that can be seen flying near water. They are harmless to humans, although big dragonflies can nip if you hold them. Dragonflies are a fearsome **predator** of flying insects and other small animals, such as fish. They glide over water or dart about, grabbing **prey** quickly from the air.

Dragonflies are such efficient killers that they capture more than nine out of every ten animals that they target. This is an impressive record that other predators would envy. A shark catches only about half of the prey it hunts, and a lion catches around one quarter of its prey.

Some adult dragonflies live for just a few weeks but others can live for up to a year.

Dragonflies are one of the deadliest predators on the planet.

Dragonflies were some of the first winged insects on Earth, around 300 million years ago. They were much bigger and scarier than dragonflies today because they had **wingspans** of up to 2 feet (60 cm) wide.

63

The Body

Like all insects, the dragonfly has six legs and a body made up of three main parts: head, **thorax**, and **abdomen**. The thorax is very strong and full of muscles. It controls the head, wing, and leg movements. The abdomen is long and thin. It gives the dragonfly its characteristic shape. Dragonflies breathe through holes in the abdomen and **digest** food there.

Superpowers

Some female dragonflies have a sharp tool with saw-like edges at the end of their abdomen. It is called an **ovipositor**. They use the ovipositor to cut slits in the stems or leaves of water plants so that they can lay their eggs inside. Imagine if humans had a body part that could work like a chainsaw to cut up trees.

64

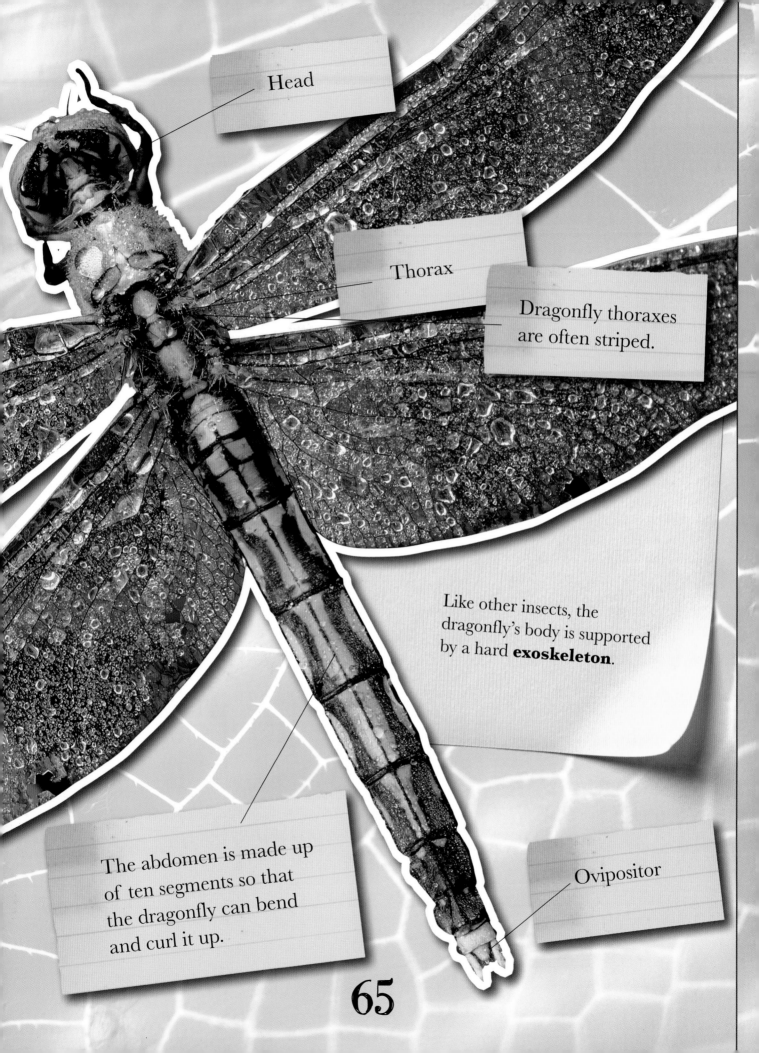

Head

Thorax

Dragonfly thoraxes are often striped.

Like other insects, the dragonfly's body is supported by a hard **exoskeleton**.

The abdomen is made up of ten segments so that the dragonfly can bend and curl it up.

Ovipositor

65

The Head

A dragonfly's head is round. It perches at the end of the dragonfly's neck so that it can swivel around easily. The dragonfly's huge eyes take up most of the head. The two bristly **antennae** are small and can be difficult to see. They are **sense organs**. They help the dragonfly to measure the speed and direction of the wind so that it can chase its victims in the air.

Superpowers

A dragonfly's huge, bulging eyes give it a 360-degree view of the world. Dragonflies can see forward and backward, and above and underneath themselves to spot prey and predators, such as birds, fish, frogs, and lizards. If humans had eyes like these, they would wrap around their head like an astronaut's helmet. They would then be able to see in all directions.

66

Eyes

Dragonfly eyes are so big that they often touch at the top of the head.

The antennae are small because dragonflies rely more on their eyes to find prey.

Some dragonflies use their huge eyes to help them to hunt at dusk when there is little light.

The Eyes

The dragonfly's two **compound eyes** give it excellent eyesight. It uses its eyes to find and catch small insects in the air and to spot predators. A dragonfly sees movements as if they are in slow motion. For example, it can see the separate beats of an insect's rapidly beating wings, which look like a blur to humans.

Superpowers

Each dragonfly eye is made up of almost 30,000 individual facets. Each facet contains a tiny *lens*. The dragonfly brain combines thousands of images from the lenses into one whole image. Dragonflies can see *ultraviolet (UV) light*, which is invisible to the human eye, and colors far beyond the range that humans can normally see.

The many facets of the compound eyes are packed side by side into a tight honeycomb formation.

Each facet points in a slightly different direction, to give the dragonfly a wide field of view.

68

Dragonflies also have three smaller eyes called ocelli.

The ocelli can detect movement more quickly than the huge compound eyes can.

A dragonfly's eyes help it to target a single animal within a swarm, while at the same time, it can see the rest of the insects to avoid crashing into them.

69

The Mouth

A dragonfly often eats its dinner in mid-air without stopping to land. One reason it can do this is because its **hinged** jaws can open as wide as its entire head, allowing the dragonfly to eat almost anything smaller than itself. When a dragonfly catches an insect, its jagged jaws clamp down hard and rip the prey's wings so that it cannot escape. The dragonfly quickly chews its victim into a gooey pulp and swallows it.

Superpowers

Dragonflies never seem to stop eating. They can eat hundreds of flies every day. Some dragonflies regularly eat animals that are 60 percent of their own body weight. That would be like a person eating more than 30 meals in one sitting!

70

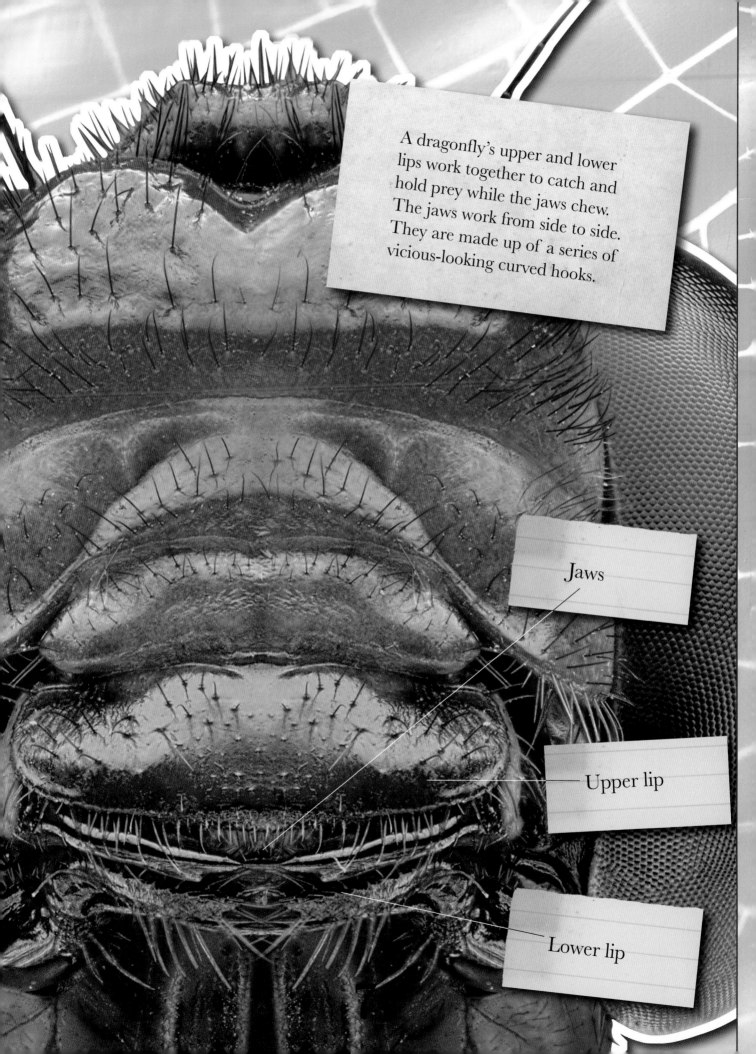

A dragonfly's upper and lower lips work together to catch and hold prey while the jaws chew. The jaws work from side to side. They are made up of a series of vicious-looking curved hooks.

Jaws

Upper lip

Lower lip

The Wings

Dragonflies have two sets of transparent wings that often have colored markings. Most dragonflies have a wingspan from 2 to 5 inches (5 to 13 cm). Dragonflies can beat each pair of wings together or separately. They can also move their back wings at a different rate from the front wings.

The largest dragonflies have a wingspan of up to 6 inches (15 cm).

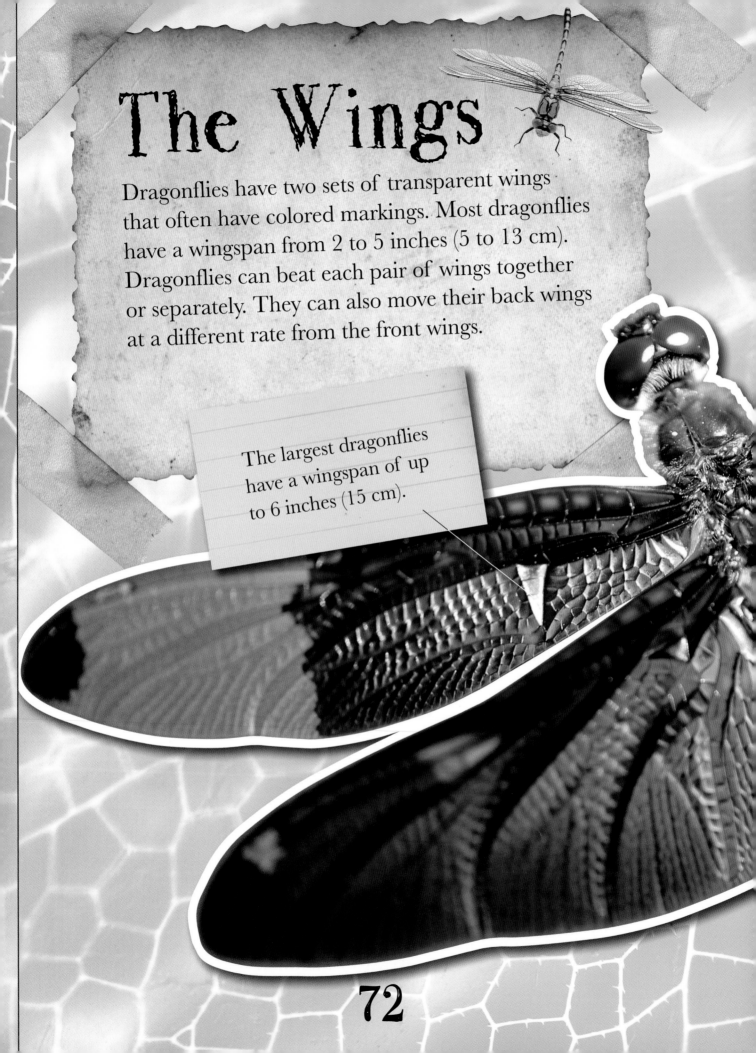

The **veins** that run through each wing give the wing strength and flexibility.

The lower wings are usually shorter and wider than the upper wings.

Superpowers

A dragonfly does not just fly forward. It can change direction in mid-air and fly left and right or backward. It can also hover on the spot. This is because its wings can beat and twist independently of each other, rather like a helicopter's blades. Just imagine if humans could take off straight up into the air and fly in all directions!

73

In Flight

A dragonfly can fly farther, higher, and faster than most other insects when on the attack. A dragonfly does not just follow its victim but works out its prey's speed and direction, so that it can intercept it in mid-air. To avoid being seen, a dragonfly attacks from below. The dragonfly keeps its head still with its eyes locked onto its target, while its body gets into the best position to attack.

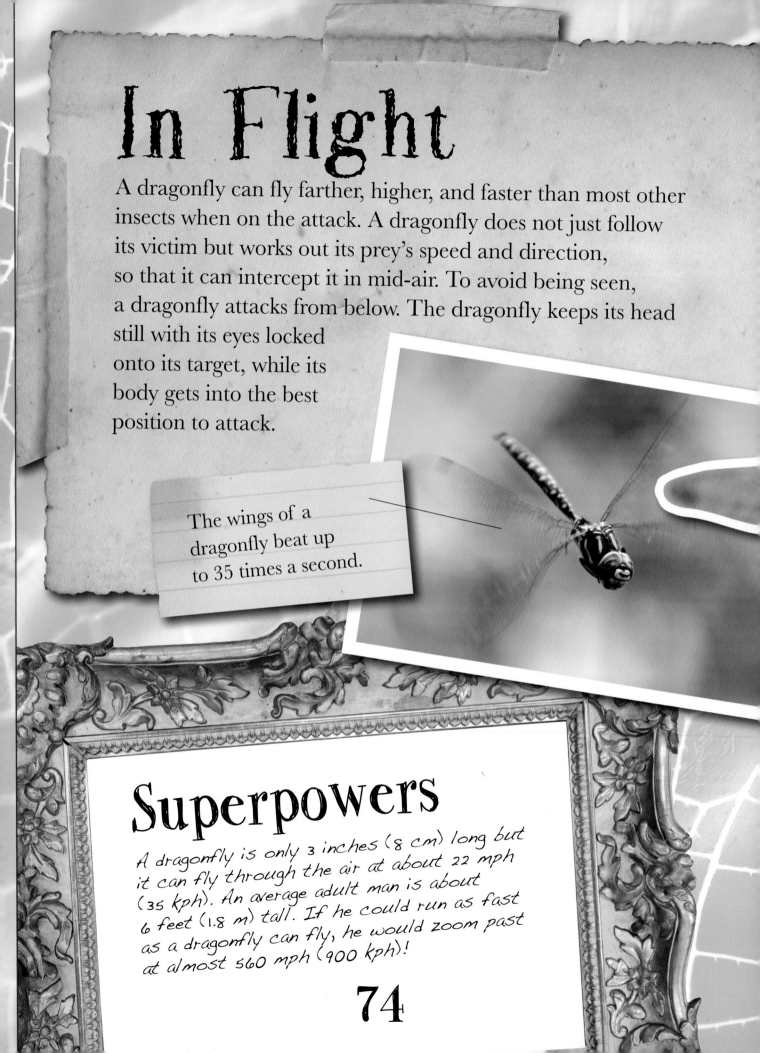

The wings of a dragonfly beat up to 35 times a second.

Superpowers

A dragonfly is only 3 inches (8 cm) long but it can fly through the air at about 22 mph (35 kph). An average adult man is about 6 feet (1.8 m) tall. If he could run as fast as a dragonfly can fly, he would zoom past at almost 560 mph (900 kph)!

The dragonfly's thorax is packed with muscles for moving the wings up and down and side to side.

Its long abdomen keeps its body balanced while maneuvering through the air.

Dragonflies are the aerial stunt artists of the insect world. Each of their four wings is controlled by different muscles, so they have perfect control over their flight.

75

The Legs

Dragonflies have six legs but they cannot walk on solid ground. They use their legs to grab their prey while flying, and to perch and balance on plants so that they can rest or feed on very large prey. Dragonflies also use their legs for grooming. Their legs have bristles that they can use like combs to rub cobwebs, dust, and water off their eyes and abdomen.

Superpowers

To catch prey, a dragonfly curves up its front legs and scoops the insect out of the air as it flies past. The bristles that cover its legs form a net to catch the insect, and a cage to trap the prey, cutting off its escape. If humans could use the hairs on their arms as giant nets, they would be able to catch and carry anything they liked.

76

Dragonflies put their legs forward to grasp vertical plant stems when they come into land. They also use their legs to catch prey.

Claw

Each of the dragonfly's legs is **jointed** so that the dragonfly can bend and curl its limbs.

Bristles

A dragonfly uses the claws at the end of each of its legs to grip its prey.

77

Nymphs

Dragonfly **larvae** are called nymphs. The nymphs hatch from eggs underwater and live in the water for a year or more. The nymphs are just as scary as their parents. They catch and eat anything that they can fit in their mouths, from small insects to tadpoles and small fish. As they grow, the nymphs **molt** many times to shed their hard outer skin. Finally, they crawl out of the water and molt one last time, emerging as an adult dragonfly with wings.

Superpowers

Nymphs breathe by taking water into their abdomen and through body parts called **gills**. They can also squeeze a jet of this water out through the end of their abdomen to make themselves shoot through the water at high speed. If humans had built-in jetpacks like these, they could shoot through the water like torpedoes!

78

Mandibles

Jaw

Mouth

Dragonfly nymphs have a long, hinged jaw with two sharp, hook-like mandibles at the end. The mandibles shoot forward and impale prey on the hooks, then pull it back into the mouth to eat it.

Green Darners

There are about 5,000 different **species**, or types, of dragonfly. The common green darner is one of the largest species. It grows up to about 3 inches (8 cm) long. Green darners can **migrate** thousands of miles from northern USA into Texas and Mexico. They travel south to lay their eggs in warmer places. These dragonflies are scary predators, capable of killing a hummingbird.

The bright green head, thorax, and abdomen of this dragonfly **camouflage** it against plants.

The green darner's wings are clear but they turn a honey-yellow color as it gets older.

80

Superpowers

Female common green darners can disappear! Well, not completely, but when they stop flying and land on a plant, they are almost impossible to see. Their green and brown body blends in with the leaves and stems, providing them with camouflage that hides them from hungry predators. If humans could blend in with a background, they too could disappear whenever they wanted.

The green darner sometimes turns a grayish or even purple color when it gets cold. Scientists think that this helps it to absorb more warmth from the sun.

The green darner is named for its very long, thin abdomen that looks like a darning needle.

Dragonhunters

Dragonhunters are as scary to dragonflies as they are to other prey. They are vicious predators that feed on other dragonflies, as well as butterflies and other large insects. Their abdomen has a very large end, known as the "club," which is usually larger in the male than in the female. These dragonflies are often brown or black, with yellow or green markings for camouflage.

Club

Superpowers

Some scientists believe that dragonhunters use their club to mimic scorpions or tree snakes to scare away predators. If humans had this superpower, they could pretend to be scarier people or animals to keep themselves out of harm's way.

Large body

The dragonhunter is a monster dragonfly! It grows to more than 3.5 inches (9 cm) long.

Small head

Long, powerful legs and wings

83

That's Scary!

Dragonflies are perfect killing machines but that is not the scariest thing about them. The truly scary thing about dragonflies is that some species are dying out, which is bad news for people.

Some species are dying out because there are fewer **wetland habitats**, as people fill in ponds and lakes to build houses or to create farmland. **Pollution** and farm chemicals, such as **insecticides**, also kill dragonflies. Dragonflies are very sensitive to changes in temperature, so they will not be able to survive heatwaves or heavy rains that may come with **climate change**.

Dragonflies help people in important ways. They are amazing pest controllers because they eat so many mosquitoes and other biting insects. Not only can biting insects be annoying, but some also spread deadly diseases. For example, mosquitoes spread malaria, which kills hundreds of thousands of people each year. Dragonflies also eat aphids, which are tiny insects that can destroy crops and other plants.

Dragonflies are important and valuable insects because they help to control populations of harmful insects around the world.

Dragonflies might look scary close up, but these beautiful insects are our friends, not our enemies.

A dragonfly can eat hundreds of mosquitoes in a single day.

85

Chapter Four:
Spiders

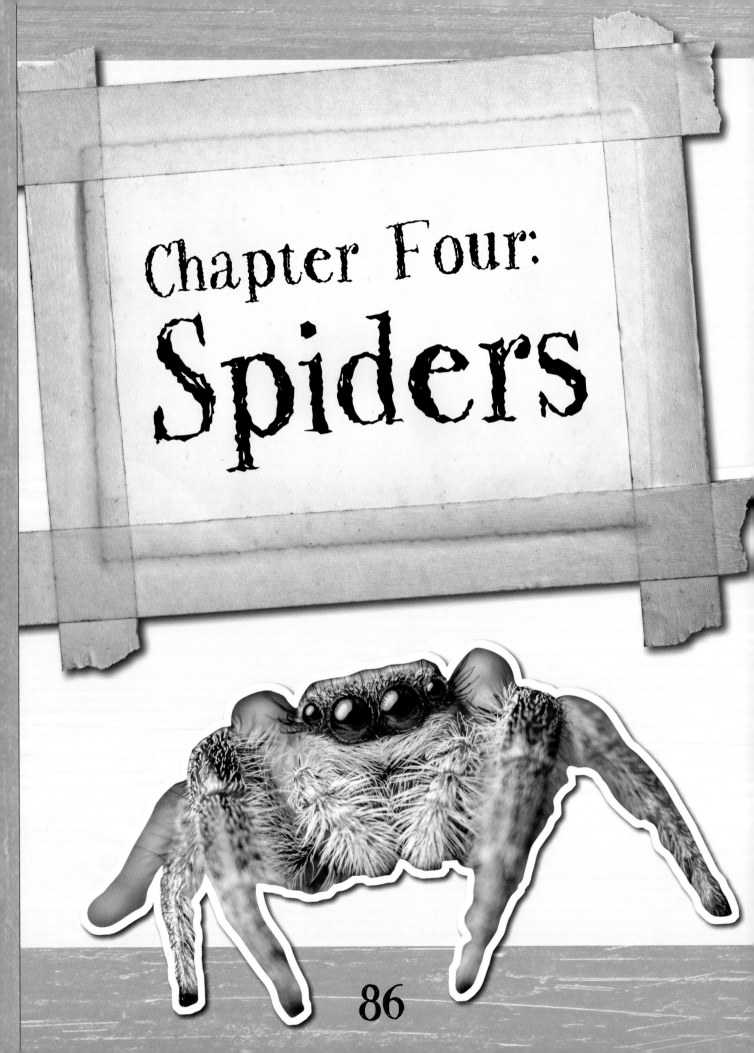

Spiders

Spiders are eight-legged **invertebrates** with a killer instinct. Their best known way of catching their prey is to spin a **silk** web. Once the prey is stuck in the web, the spider rushes out and bites its victim with its fearsome **fangs**. This stops the prey from moving. The spider then starts to eat the creature at its leisure. Some spiders do not spin webs. These scary hunters give chase or lie in wait before ambushing their victims, taking them by surprise.

Some adult spiders are as tiny as a pinhead and you would need a magnifying glass to spot them. Others are as big as dinner plates. Worldwide, there are more than 40,000 different species, or types, of spiders. Some types can give humans a painful nip and others can kill people! Although spiders mostly do not harm people, some of us find them very scary.

Silk web

Spiders are some of the world's deadliest and scariest **predators**.

Fang

Spiders have two main parts to their bodies, and eight legs. They never have wings. They are different from insects. Insects have three body parts, six legs, and sometimes have wings.

The Body

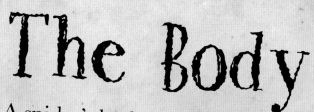

A spider's body has two parts. The cephalothorax is the front part. It is like a head and a **thorax** joined together. The spider's eyes, mouth, and thin legs are on the outside of the cephalothorax, and the brain is inside. The abdomen is the fatter part at the rear of the spider. It is connected to the cephalothorax by a thin waist, or pedicel. Spiders digest food, produce silk, and make eggs in their abdomen.

Superpowers

An adult female Brazilian wandering spider can produce more than 1,000 eggs in her abdomen. She lays the eggs and spins a silk **egg sac** around them for protection. The eggs hatch inside the egg sac. The tiny spiders stay there safely until they are ready to start hunting for food. Then, they spill out. Imagine if one human could produce hundreds of babies at a time!

90

Most spiders breathe in air through tiny holes near the end of their abdomen. The holes connect to a network of tubes called **tracheae**. Tracheae carry oxygen through the spider's body for **respiration**.

Abdomen

Cephalothorax

Inside the cephalothorax are the muscles that make the spider's legs move.

Pedicel

Some spiders' brains are as small as a poppy seed, but other spiders have bigger brains that take up a lot of room in the cephalothorax, and even spill into their legs.

91

Hairs

Many spiders are hairy—very hairy! These hairs are not for keeping the spider warm. Instead, they provide vital information. Some hairs can detect tiny **vibrations** in the air. A spider has thousands of these hairs that, together, function a bit like human ears. They help the spider to hear the type of prey moving nearby. They also enable the spider to keep its balance. Other hairs detect chemicals, such as those released by other spiders.

Superpowers

If a tarantula feels threatened or angry and it turns its abdomen toward you, watch out! The spider can kick its legs at the top of its abdomen to send out a cloud of hairs. Each hair is filled with an irritating chemical and has a barbed tip, like a harpoon. The hairs stick in the skin and release the chemical, which can irritate eyes and cause itching skin. If humans had this superpower, their body hairs could be aimed at other people like darts.

Hair

Abdomen

Leg

Watch out for spiders with no hair on the back of their abdomen. It could mean they have been kicking off hairs for defense, and might do so again.

93

The Eyes

One of the scary things about spiders is their beady black eyes. Spiders usually have eight eyes that are arranged over the top, front, and sides of the cephalothorax so they can see all around them. Spiders can have six, four, or two eyes. Sometimes, the eyes are of different sizes. The bigger **primary eyes** can see things clearly. The smaller **secondary eyes** can only spot the difference between light and dark or day and night.

Superpowers

Jumping spiders have the sharpest vision of all spiders. The two primary eyes are extra-large and close together. These can see objects in detail from 12 inches (30 cm) away and spot things moving at twice this distance. If these spiders were human sized, they could see in detail from a distance of 98 feet (30 meters).

94

Primary eye

Secondary eye

Mouthpart

Leg

The jumping spider's large primary eyes have a small **field of vision** but they are mounted close together. They give the spider a clear view of prey and help it to figure out how far to jump to catch it.

The Fangs

One of the most terrifying parts of a spider is its fangs. These pointed prongs are its main weapon. When a spider's fangs pierce its victim, they squirt in venom, or poison. The venom **paralyzes** the prey. The spider's mouth is just beneath the fangs and can only suck in food. So, when it is ready to eat, the spider sprays digestive juices from its fangs to **dissolve** its prey into a mushy liquid ready to suck into its stomach.

Superpowers

The wandering spider has the most poisonous venom of any spider. The venom is squirted from large venom **glands** in its cephalothorax. These glands are around 0.4 inches (10 mm) long and hold enough venom to kill 225 mice. If this spider were to bite you, you would experience intense pain, sweating, shivering, and have difficulty breathing. Luckily, there are special medicines to stop the effects of this venom.

96

Most spiders cannot bite people because they are unable to pierce human skin with their tiny fangs.

Fangs can fold back into pouches in the spider's mouthparts to keep them out of the way.

The spider's fangs are curved inward to help it to grip its prey while it is injecting venom.

Fang

97

The Pedipalps

The pedipalps at the front of the cephalothorax are often mistaken for an extra set of legs, but they are actually mouthparts with **joints**. Spiders use pedipalps to capture and hold prey, and to help to wrap their prey in silk. They use them as feelers and to shape their webs. In male spiders, the pedipalps usually have clubbed ends. These are used during **reproduction**.

Fang

Joint

Pedipalp

People can be confused because pedipalps can look so much like legs that they think they have seen a ten-legged spider!

Eye

Pedipalp

Superpowers

Spiders will attack prey much larger than themselves. Once, a whistling tarantula measuring 8.7 inches (22 cm) wide, killed a hen and dragged it 52.5 feet (16 meters) to its hole, with the help of its pedipalps. That is like a man dragging a cow ten times that distance with his teeth!

99

The Legs

The very thought of a spider crawling over them is enough to make some people terrified. Spiders always have eight legs. Each leg is made up of seven parts or segments. The segment at the tip, called the tarsus, has tiny claws to help the spider to grip onto things. It also has tufts of hairs with flattened parts. These special hairs can stick to most surfaces, even bathtubs, and stop the spider slipping as it moves.

The seven segments of the leg are the coxa (attached to the cephalothorax), trochanter, femur, patella, tibia, metatarsus, and tarsus.

Superpowers

Spiders can move their legs very fast. Some can run a distance of 70 times their body length in one second. That would be like running ten times faster than Usain Bolt, the fastest sprinter in the world! Luckily this scary feat is short-lived because spiders can run this fast for only a few seconds at a time.

100

Coxa

Trochanter

Femur

Patella

Tibia

Metatarsus

Tarsus

Cellar spiders have very long legs compared to their body size, but other spiders have shorter legs relative to their bodies.

The Spinnerets

The cone-shaped bumps at the back end of a spider's abdomen are called **spinnerets**. These special parts are used for spinning silk. The silk is a liquid made in large silk glands inside the spider's abdomen. The silk is squeezed out from tiny holes in the spinnerets, like toothpaste from a tube. The silk hardens into narrow strands of silk fiber as it comes out.

Superpowers

Silk is one of nature's most incredible materials. It is stretchy and elastic, and even those very thin strands in spiderwebs, or the lines they spin to lower themselves to the ground, are very strong. A strand the thickness of a pencil would be extremely strong—strong enough to even stop a jumbo jet in flight!

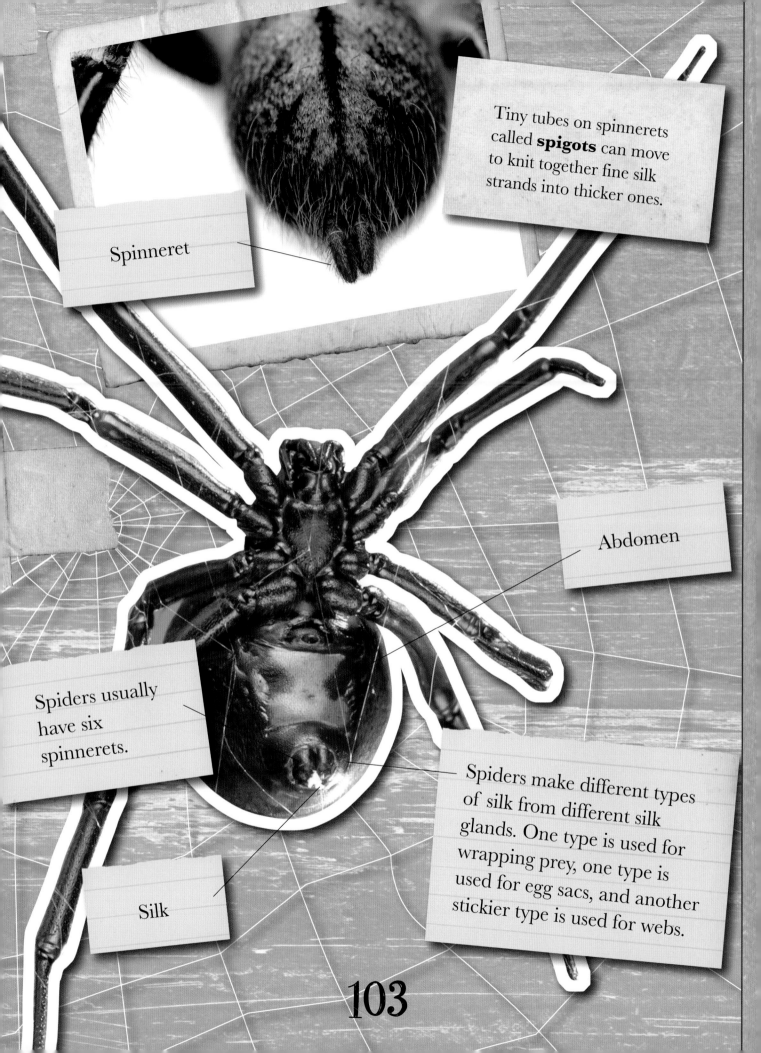

Tiny tubes on spinnerets called **spigots** can move to knit together fine silk strands into thicker ones.

Spinneret

Abdomen

Spiders usually have six spinnerets.

Silk

Spiders make different types of silk from different silk glands. One type is used for wrapping prey, one type is used for egg sacs, and another stickier type is used for webs.

Web Builders

Many of the world's spiders build webs to catch flying prey, which is mostly insects. Web spinners start with one long horizontal silk line or **frame thread**, attached between two firm supports, such as branches. They then start to add more frame threads to build the outer lines of the web. Spiders span the center of the web with **radius threads**. Finally, they run an **auxiliary spiral** of sticky threads from the edge of the web toward the center.

Superpowers

Have you ever seen movies where people wander into and get caught in giant spiderwebs? That might be possible in the Darwin's bark spider's web. This spider's web is 10 feet (3 meters) in diameter and is part of a silk structure spanning widths of up to 82 feet (25 meters). Thankfully, this spider is only around 0.6 inches (1.5 cm) wide and is not at all interested in people. It builds its super web over rivers in order to catch flying insects.

Radius thread

Auxiliary spiral

Web builders have oily feet that allow them to walk on the sticky auxiliary spiral.

Spiders rest on their webs, waiting to feel the vibrations as an insect gets stuck on it. They move quickly to the prey, paralyze it, and either eat it then and there, or wrap it in silk to save for later.

Hunting Spiders

Hunting spiders are fearsome predators, rather like mini eight-legged wolves! They are built for fast ground assault with heavier legs, bigger eyes, and tougher fangs for chewing than web builders. Some hunting spiders, such as wolf spiders, move around in search of prey and give chase. Other hunters remain in hiding until passing prey comes close by. Crab spiders are **camouflaged** in exactly the same color as the plants they rest on, while trapdoor spiders stay out of sight in a hole ready to pounce on passing victims.

Trapdoor

Leg

Fang

Eye

Superpowers

Jumping spiders leap by using a powerful muscle in their cephalothorax. The muscle squirts fluids from their body into their legs to make them stiffen and push them off the ground. These spiders can jump 50 times their body length to catch prey. That is equivalent to a human long-jumper leaping 295 feet (90 meters) without a run up!

Trapdoor spiders dig holes, cover them up with dirt doors hinged with spider silk, and lie in wait for passing prey.

Jumping spiders prey on worms and insects such as flies, shield bugs, and mosquitoes.

Prey

Spiderlings

Baby spiders, or spiderlings, look exactly like their parents. They can hunt or build webs in the same pattern as the adults, too. As they eat and grow bigger, the tough **exoskeleton** around their bodies cannot grow with them. Instead, it splits open, they climb out and puff up, and a new bigger exoskeleton forms. This is called **molting**. Spiderlings are small and light enough to balloon in the wind. The wind blows them away from where they hatched to new places to live.

Superpowers

Spiderlings balloon by climbing to high spots, such as treetops, before pointing their spinnerets in the direction of the wind. The breeze blows out a line of silk, which pulls the spiderlings high in the air. Tiny spiderlings can balloon for hundreds of miles at a height of more than 1 mile (1.6 km) for up to 25 days at a time. No wonder spiders are found on every continent on Earth.

108

Spiderlings bunch together for safety, but will scatter apart if they are disturbed.

Spiderling

Silk thread

Sometimes, millions of spiderlings will balloon at the same time and land in one area, coating it with silk threads.

109

That's Scary!

With their sticky webs, extra eyes, hair darts, fangs, and paralyzing venom, spiders are some of the scariest predators. However, spiders are also amazing creatures with remarkable abilities, from silk weaving and ballooning to pest control.

Spiders also play a vital role in the natural world. They are predators of insects that can damage plants and spread disease. Spiders are also an important food for some animals. Some birds, such as hummingbirds, use spider silk to line their nests. Without spiders, just imagine how many more flies would be in our homes, and how many more bugs there would be to eat food crops.

The really scary thing about spiders is that people are putting them under threat. Pollution and farm chemicals, such as **insecticides**, are killing spiders. **Deforestation** and **climate change** caused by human activities is disrupting their lives and destroying their habitats. By caring better for our planet, we will be looking after spiders and enabling them to carry on their good work.

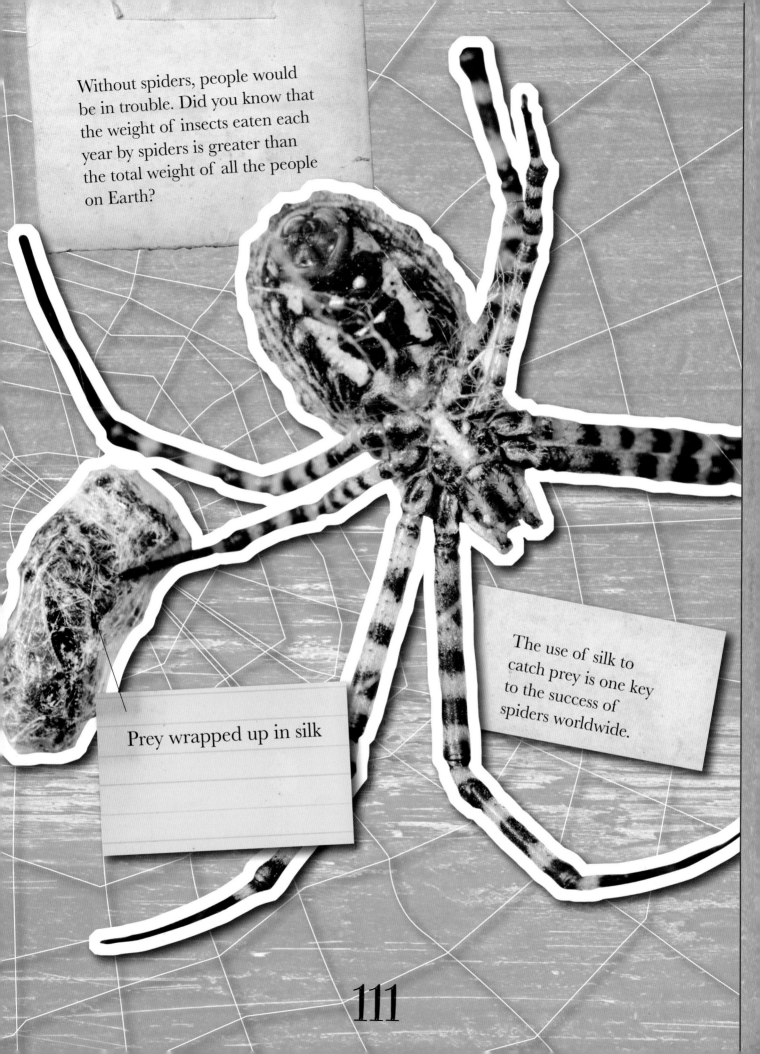

Without spiders, people would be in trouble. Did you know that the weight of insects eaten each year by spiders is greater than the total weight of all the people on Earth?

Prey wrapped up in silk

The use of silk to catch prey is one key to the success of spiders worldwide.

Chapter Five: Frightening Fun

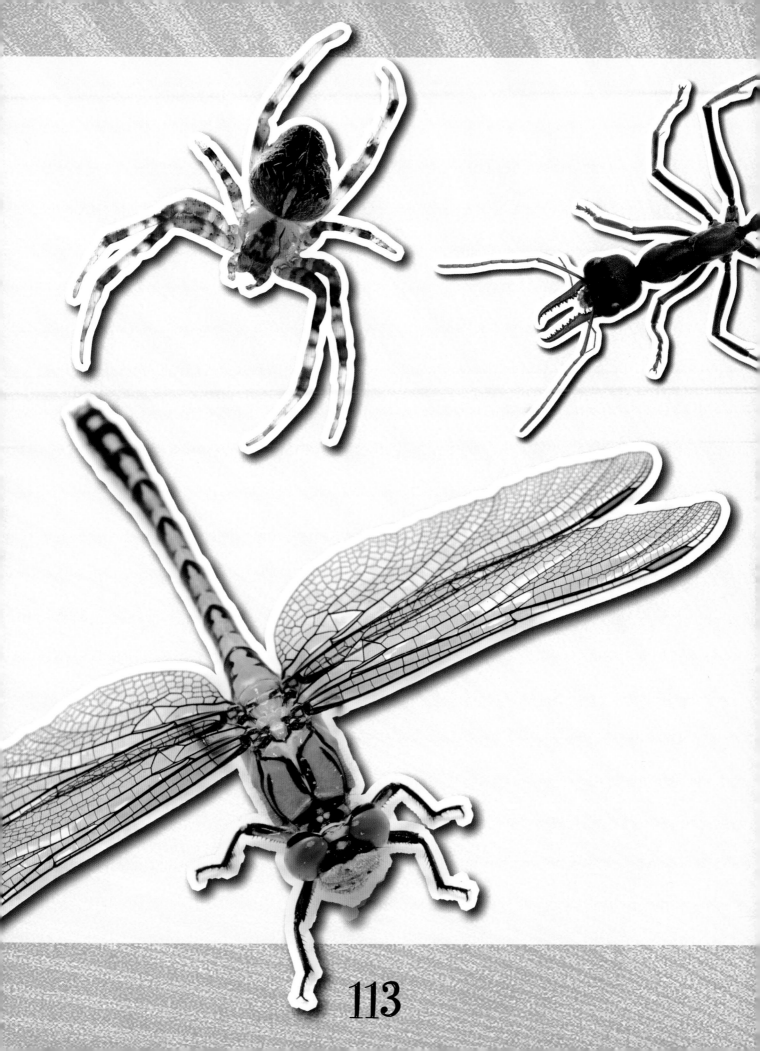

113

What Do Bugs Do For Us?

It's a bug eat bug world out there—and this is good for us. Insect species that prey on crop-eating pests save farmers from relying so much on harmful chemicals to control population levels.

Insects recycle waste products from humans and other life forms. Dung beetles eat the excrement left behind by other animals, or roll it away and lay their eggs inside so that the larvae have a food source when they hatch. Other insect species eat rotten wood and dead leaves. Without this recycling process, the world would be swamped by waste.

Scientists have learned new design skills by watching different species of insects at work. By observing the way that termites build their enormous nests to keep them cool, experts are developing their ability to regulate the temperature in human-sized buildings using less energy.

Insects have also been used in medicine and surgery. Blowfly maggots are introduced to infected wounds so that the larvae can release chemicals that digest and destroy bacteria or dead organic tissue. This helps to keep the patient healthy.

Leeches have been used throughout human history in medical treatments, mainly to remove blood from patients. Today, leeches are still used in some forms of micro and plastic surgery to reduce blood congestion in veins around the area of the operation.

Humans eat insects too! In many parts of the world, insects are considered a delicacy and are sold to hungry customers as a snack. Scientists are also developing ways of using insect meat to replace meat from animal livestock, since insects are low in fat, high in protein and nutrients, and much cheaper to farm.

Scary Statistics

Over 1 million people die from illnesses carried by mosquitoes every year.

The Brazilian wandering spider and Australian funnel web spider are the only two species of spider whose venom is lethal to humans.

Bee populations are shrinking rapidly. More than 40 percent of all honeybee colonies in the United States were lost between 2014 and 2015 alone.

The Goliath beetle is the world's heaviest insect. Growing to over 4 inches (10 cm) long, it can weigh up to 3.5 ounces (100 grams).

Mayflies have the shortest lifespan of any animal, living for only 24 hours. The Dolania americana has the shortest lifespan of any mayfly, with the adult female living for only 5 minutes!

A species of Australian tiger beetle called Cicindela hudsoni is the fastest insect in the world. It can run 8.2 feet (2.5 meters) in a second. At that speed, the beetle's eyesight cannot keep up and it becomes temporarily blind.

Queen Alexandra's Birdwing is the world's largest butterfly. It has a wingspan of 11 inches (28 cm).

The highest-jumping insect, relative to its size, is the froghopper. At only 0.2 inches (5 mm) long, it can jump up to 28 inches (71 cm) from plant to plant.

The male African cicada is the world's loudest insect. The mating calls it makes by vibrating its muscles can reach a volume of 110 decibels from 20 inches (50 cm) away—louder than a jet passing overhead!

The Peruvian giant yellowleg is the world's largest centipede. It grows up to 12 inches (30.5 cm) in length and is a highly aggressive predator. It has been known to eat bats, mice, lizards, and frogs.

The brightest insect is the Jamaican click beetle. It has two lights on either side of its head that glow bright green continuously to attract mates.

Swallowtail butterflies are some of the best imitators in the whole of the animal kingdom. They can mimic other species of butterfly in more than 30 ways, including how they smell and taste food.

Creepy-crawlies Quiz

It's time to test your knowledge!
How much do you remember?

1. What is the name for a spider's jointed mouthparts?

2. Which part of its body does a dragonfly breathe through?

3. What do bees feed to a larva that has been chosen as the next queen?

4. What species of ant can lift up to 100 times its own body weight?

5. What kind of light can bees see that humans can't?

6. How do dragonfly nymphs move through water?

7. What is the name of an ant's strong, jagged jaws?

8. Roughly how many ants are there on the planet?

9. How do spiderlings travel away from the nest where they're born?

10. What is the wingspan of the largest living dragonflies?

11. How long can a bee's tongue be?

12. How many times its body length can a jumping spider jump?

13. How many millions of years ago did dragonflies first evolve?

14. What two species were crossbred to make killer bees?

15. What do a spider's hairs help it to detect?

16. What is the name of the hexagonal units in a bee's compound eyes?

Answers

1. Pedipalps

2. The abdomen

3. Royal jelly

4. Weaver ant

5. Ultraviolet (UV) light

6. By expelling a jet of water from its abdomen.

7. Mandibles

8. 100 trillion

9. By ballooning on a line of silk blown by the breeze.

10. 6 inches (15 cm)

11. 0.8 inches (2 cm)

12. 50 times its body length

13. Approximately 300 million years ago

14. European honeybees and African bees

15. Vibrations in the air

16. Ommatidia

Glossary

Abdomen the part of an insect's body farthest from its head.

Antennae a pair of sense organs located near the front of an insect's head.

Auxiliary spiral the coiled part of a spider's web that forms rings.

Camouflaged hidden using a color or shape that is similar to the background.

Chemical a substance made by a chemical process.

Climate change the gradual increase in Earth's temperature, thought to be caused by human actions such as burning oil, gas, and coal.

Colony a group of animals of the same type that live together in one place.

Compound eyes eyes made up of many lenses.

Currents movements of water or air in particular directions.

Deforestation cutting down forests, usually to create farmland or to uncover land for mining.

Digest to break down food to be absorbed into the body.

Dissolve to break down a solid into a liquid.

Egg sac a silk structure that encloses and protects eggs.

Exoskeleton the hard outer covering on the outside of some animals' bodies.

Fangs curved spike-shaped mouthparts on some animals that usually can inject venom into prey.

Field of vision what is possible to see.

Formic acid a type of smelly and burning chemical.

Frame thread the outer framework of a spider's web that supports the inner radius threads and auxiliary spiral.

Gills the body parts that dragonfly nymphs, fish, and some other animals use to breathe underwater.

Glands body parts that produce special chemicals, such as venom or silk, with particular functions.

Habitats the places where an animal or plant usually lives.

Hinged joined so that it opens and closes like a door.

Hives nests built by bees.

Honeycomb a structure of hexagonal cells of wax that forms the inside of a hive.

Insecticides chemicals sprayed on plants to kill plant-eating insects that can also harm other living things.

Invertebrates a group of animals without backbones, ranging from slugs and worms to insects.

Jointed having two separately moving bones or body parts that meet, like at the knee joint on a human leg.

Larvae the wingless, often worm-like, form of insects when they first hatch from eggs.

Lens the part of an eye that gathers light so an animal can see.

Magnetic field the area around a magnetic object where magnetic forces can be felt. Earth has a magnetic field because it contains magnetic metals in its core.

Mandibles jaws.

Mate the way animals create new versions of themselves.

Glossary continued

Migrate to move from one place to another in different seasons.

Mites small animals related to spiders.

Molt to shed hair or skin.

Ommatidia the units that make up a compound eye.

Organic matter part of soil formed from the remains of living things and their waste.

Ovipositor a body part that female insects use to lay eggs.

Pheromones chemicals that are released to send signals to other animals.

Pollinate when pollen from one flower moves to another flower of the same kind to make seeds and develop fruit.

Pollution something found in water, air, or land that damages it or makes it harmful to living things.

Predators animals that catch other animals to eat.

Primary eyes the largest pair of eyes on some spiders, often with the clearest vision.

Prey animal eaten by others.

Radius threads inner part of a spider's web that look like spokes on a bicycle wheel.

Ratio the relationship that exists between the size, number, or amount of two things.

Reproduction the way that living things create new versions of themselves.

Respiration using energy from food to power body processes such as growth. In many living things, respiration requires oxygen that is breathed in as part of air.

Secondary eyes the smallest eyes on a spider capable only of detecting light and dark.

Sense organs body parts that give an animal one or more of the five senses. The five senses are sight, hearing, smell, taste, and touch.

Silk a strong, elastic material that spiders and some other invertebrates produce.

Simple eyes eyes with only one lens.

Species a group of living things that are similar in many ways and can reproduce with each other.

Spigots tiny moveable tubes on the spinneret that squeeze out silk.

Spinnerets the body parts of a spider that weave silk from glands into threads.

Stinger the body part at the end of the abdomen that injects or sprays venom.

Thorax the body part between the head and abdomen with legs attached to it.

Tracheae strengthened tubes for moving air through some animals' insides for breathing.

Ultraviolet (UV) light a form of light energy that humans cannot see.

Venom poisonous fluid used to kill prey but also to warn off predators.

Vibration A rapid movement back and forth or side to side.

Wetland land saturated by water most or all of the time, such as a swamp, marsh, pond, or lake.

Wingspan the total width of the wings from the tip of one wing to the tip of the other.

Worker bees the female bees that do all the work in a colony.

Index